BRIGITTA,

LITTLE GIRL IN THE ALLEGHENY MOUNTAINS

GROWING UP IN THE 1940'S

INGE LOGENBURG KYLER

authorHOUSE®

AuthorHouse™
1663 Liberty Drive
Bloomington, IN 47403
www.authorhouse.com
Phone: 1 (800) 839-8640

Published by AuthorHouse 01/29/2019

ISBN: 978-1-5462-7781-1 (sc)
ISBN: 978-1-5462-7780-4 (e)

Library of Congress Control Number: 2019900928

Print information available on the last page.

This book is printed on acid-free paper.

Contents

Chapter 1   The Mishap..1

Chapter 2   The Spelling Bee 5

Chapter 3   The Troublesome Name..7

Chapter 4   Down in the Valley..9

Chapter 5   The Playhouse..12

Chapter 6   Dancing School 16

Chapter 7   Realization..21

Chapter 8   Things to Do 24

Chapter 9   The Little Bungalow 28

Chapter 10   Settlements Over the Mountain................................31

Chapter 11   Other Country Roads..34

Chapter 12   Neighboring Farmhouses...37

Chapter 13   Playmates..42

Chapter 14   Coal Mining Towns.. 44

Chapter 15   Grandmother's House...48

Chapter 16   Trips to Coalport 51

Chapter 17   Electricity Comes to the Valley 53

Chapter 18   Brigitta's Father...56

Chapter 19   Farm Animals...60

Chapter 20   Valentine's Day..63

Chapter 21 The Horrible Accident...65

Chapter 22 World War II..67

Chapter 23 The Circus 70

Chapter 24 Summer Vacation 72

Dedicated to Cecilia Violet Dickerson

They send forth their little ones like a flock,
and their children dance. Job 21:11

Chapter 1

The Mishap

The bright copper-colored corduroy skirt seemed much too hot for such a warm stuffy day. Today was the first day of school and Brigitta had been looking forward to being able to wear her brand new skirt that reminded her of maple leaves in October. She knew the skirt might be too hot for September, but she wanted to wear it anyway.

Despite the room being warm, the school windows were closed. There was not even a bit of a breeze. Brigitta began to feel uncomfortable and started squirming in her seat, and wished she was outdoors instead of in this stuffy room.

Suddenly, someone was calling her name, "Brigitta! Brigitta." A sea of faces were swarming around her and she felt herself being caught in a black cylinder that was swirling around and around! The faces seemed to be kind and familiar. She tried to reach out and touch them, but voices faintly called, "Go back! Go back!"

She felt herself being drawn down, down, down, swirling and whirling until suddenly it felt like a weight had been lifted off of her. Startled, she opened her eyes to see her teacher, Mrs. Winters, peering down at her, calling her name.

Brigitta found herself on a cot in the hallway of Plymptonville

1

Elementary School. Mrs. Winters was her fourth grade teacher, and right now had a most worried look on her face. "It's all right, Brigitta," she said. "Apparently you fainted and bumped your head against the desk beside you. How do you feel?"

Fainted, Brigitta thought, in front of the whole school? How embarrassing was that! Well, it was Mrs. Winters' fault for forcing her to sit up ramrod straight for penmanship class on such a hot day! Mrs. Winters had snapped the ruler on her fingers when she had slumped a bit in her chair.

The rule for writing class was that students must sit up straight and tall and never slump. Each student had to hold his left hand on the paper in a certain manner, and was instructed to hold pencils in the right hand between the thumb and forefinger. The right elbow had to firmly hold down the writing paper. Anyone who did not follow those rules, had his fingers snapped by the ruler.

No, it wasn't her fault she fainted! It was all because of Mrs. Winters and her stern rules! Brigitta kept these thoughts to herself as she heard Mrs. Winters say, "Well, never mind. I'll have Principal Fuller drive you home. Is your mother home during the day?" Mrs. Winters sounded very annoyed at this interruption in her orderly day.

"Yes, Mrs. Winters," Brigitta weakly replied, realizing to her dismay that her underpants felt wet. Do all people who faint wet their pants, she wondered? She felt mortified and was glad she was on a cot in the hall and not in the classroom. What were her classmates saying or thinking? She couldn't wait to get home.

As she sat in Principal Fuller's car on the way home, she wondered why she should have to faint, in order to be so privileged to ride in Principal Fuller's car. She sat quietly as they drove through the narrow streets of Plymptonville.

Soon they were following the winding Susquehanna River as they drove up and down hills to Brigitta's home. The river was low at this time of year due to unusually hot weather. Rocks and sand were visible in many places that usually were covered with water.

Finally, they turned off the paved highway onto a curving dirt road and drove past thick woods on one side and a wide meadow full of white heath daisies on the other. Soon they came to a little red bungalow.

Brigitta's mother was on the porch when they drove up. When she saw her, she hurried out. "Brigitta, is everything all right?"

"I felt sick to the stomach and I guess I fainted," she said. She hadn't really felt sick, but it sounded good. She didn't want to blame Mrs. Winters for her mean strict class rules, and yet she did.

"Thank you, Principal Fuller, for bringing Brigitta home," said her mother as Brigitta made her way into the house.

"Oh, it's all right, Mrs. Logan" said Principal Fuller, in a manner which Brigitta felt was not all right! Principal Fuller stepped back into the blue humped Plymouth and soon was driving back up the winding road.

"Maybe you should lie down for awhile," said Brigitta's mother. Her mother was never overly concerned if anyone in the house got sick. She just didn't believe in sickness. There was too much to do, it seemed, and being sick meant nothing could get done.

Brigitta remembered when she came down with measles and her mother paid no attention until she noticed a bunch of red spots on her face. Her mother had to walk across the field to Farmer Brown's house to use their telephone to call the doctor since there was no telephone in their own house.

The doctor had come right out that night and had shone a flashlight in her face as he checked her over. "Yep, measles," he said, and told her mother to keep her quiet in bed in a dark room with blinds pulled in order to protect her eyes.

Brigitta had to stay in bed for a week. The week seemed like an eternity. But today she felt upset with herself for fainting and having to be taken home. Maybe she shouldn't have worn such a heavy skirt on such a hot day. Maybe, but soon her eyes felt heavy, and she fell sound asleep.

Chapter 2

The Spelling Bee

"Didn't that hurt?" asked Tommy, a skinny boy in baggy long pants. "You hit your head on the edge of my desk," Tommy went on, pointing to the desk beside her, "so hard that I thought you might be dead! I never saw anyone faint before. How did that feel?"

Brigitta looked at him disgustingly. Boys! Why did they have to prattle so much! It was as if no one had ever fainted before, although she, herself, could not remember having ever seen anyone do it. She wondered what she looked like on the floor. She tried to dismiss it from her mind. It was too undignified to think about.

She was small for her age. In fact, she was probably one of the smallest students in her room. Her mother sewed most of her clothes as there just didn't seem to be store-bought clothing that fit her properly. They were all too big.

One good thing was that she had naturally curly hair. Sometimes her mother wound her hair in rags and when she pulled out the rags in the morning, her head would be full of long ringlets like Shirley Temple.

All mothers, it seemed, wanted their daughters to look like Shirley Temple. Shirley was a famous child movie star, and had long ringlets of curls. Sleeping with a head full of rag curls was not easy.

When she looked at herself in a mirror, she saw a little girl with features that didn't seem to look right, at least not to her! Why couldn't she have a cute little nose like some of the girls in her class?

No, she didn't like anything about her face, and wondered why the angels in Heaven sent her to earth looking like that!

Her sister had beautiful blonde hair and eyes of sky blue like her father. Well, she thought, nothing can be done about it now. I am what I am. Maybe my nose will get smaller as I grow up, she thought to herself.

Writing class today was much better than yesterday as the air had cooled somewhat. Following writing class, the music teacher would be coming to help students prepare for a performance they would be doing over the radio. That was always fun. The whole class would do a recitation.

Sometimes they held spelling bees over the radio. Only about seven students participated in that. She was one of the lucky chosen ones. Well, not all of them were lucky. Her classmates, Jack and Shirley, knew they would be in trouble at home if they misspelled any words in the radio spelling bee. They never said much but Brigitta knew that their mothers smacked their legs with sticks if they did not do well as both of them had marks on their legs when they came to school the next day.

Brigitta felt sorry for them both. Although Jack wore long pants, Brigitta knew his mother had whipped his legs, too, as he walked a little stiff when he came into the classroom the next day.

Chapter 3

The Troublesome Name

The class was so busy working on music lessons and studying spelling, that everyone had forgotten about Brigitta's mishap from the day before.

When the music teacher read off the names of those who would be performing, she stopped and hesitated when she got to Brigitta's name. No one, it seemed, knew how to pronounce it.

"Just call her Bridge," snickered Billy as he and some other boys started to laugh. Brigitta pretended she didn't hear them.

Why, oh why, did her parents give her such a name? Why didn't she get a pretty name like Mary, which was her sister's name?

But at least things were better this year than last year now that the World War II had ended. Her classmates had teased her during the war because her parents were born in Germany.

They would yell "Heil Hitler" at her at recess time on the playground. Oh, how she hated that!

Everyone knew that Germany's Adolf Hitler was the terrible man who had caused the horrible war that had been raging in Europe. It was because of him that her parents, once a week, carefully wrapped sugar, cocoa, flour and other staples in clothing and sent them to relatives who still lived in Germany.

Even though the war was over, they continued to send things since cities and villages in Germany had been badly hit by bombs from overhead aircraft, and few stores were left undamaged.

The newspapers were full of horrible pictures of the damage caused by bombings in Germany and other countries. She knew her relatives were suffering great hardships despite the fact that they had nothing to do with the war.

None of them liked Hitler or believed in what he was doing, but anyone who dared to speak against him was either thrown in prison or shot.

Both of her parents had been born in Germany and had returned to Germany soon after her sister, Mary, was born, with the intent of staying there. But her father's sisters convinced him that he needed to go back to the United States as everyone feared a war was coming. They were right.

Her father's oldest brother had died in World War I when his plane was shot down by an American pilot, and another brother had been shot down in his plane during World War II. His sisters did not want to lose another brother.

No, she hated it when her classmates teased her, but she tried hard not to let it bother her. Instead, she would pull out the journal she had started and would continue writing poems and stories.

"My name is pronounced Brig-e-tta, she would tell her teachers. She didn't like how they pronounced her name, but that was better than calling her "ridge" or "bridge."

Chapter 4

Down in the Valley

Brigitta loved the little bungalow that her father and mother had built in the Allegheny Mountains Valley. She couldn't imagine living anywhere else.

She loved how the morning fog would hang over the valley like a heavy mist covering the mountains and forests. When the fog lifted, the first rays of the sun would filter through everything like a candle in a dark room. Often a deer or two could be seen standing in the meadow or by the big apple tree.

A creek bubbled and gurgled down from the mountains and across the yard in front of their house. In the late summer ripe purple elderberries dangled over its banks. Although for the most part, the creek was shallow, her father dammed part of it for a swimming hole.

The creek was a wonderful place to splash during the hot summers. She would throw rose petals in the water and splash around like the famous movie star, Esther Williams. The creek was full of crayfish and water striders. She didn't mind them but she did not like the big water spiders that also swam in the water or hung along the banks.

Nor did she like the brown spotted water snakes that drifted along the creek banks. When she saw them, she quickly climbed out of the water even though her father told her the snakes were harmless.

The swimming area was deep enough so her mother or father could come and splash in the water, too, which they did some days.

The creek wandered into a woods that was close to her bedroom. The woods was a wonderful place to play, especially since she had discovered an old mill along the creek banks. The mill was formed from two large rocks, side by side, each hollowed out years ago with deep grooves when woodland people pounded corn.

People told her that a woodland peoples village was once on their property. Brigitta tried to imagine how those times must have been.

She used the mill to grind chokecherries for mud pies, and she gathered sticks and poles to build tepees. She loved pretending that she was a woodland people maiden dancing in the woods.

Her mother told her that woodland people had once lived in that area. That would explain the reason for the mill and all the other artifacts that were found along the creek or in the meadow.

She was also told that long ago a pioneer mother hid her baby in one of the hollowed trees in the woods to keep it safe when some woodland people suddenly appeared. People, during that time, were never sure who was friendly or not.

Brigitta loved all those stories and felt sorry for the native peoples who were pushed farther and farther away from their homeland and hunting grounds. When she found arrowheads or stone bowls in the fields and meadows she tried to imagine what life must have been like for the people who used to live in her woods and fields. The valley and hills seemed to hold mysteries everywhere she turned. She wondered about the abandoned road between her house and the woods. Where did it lead and why was it there? The road seemed to lead over the mountains but she couldn't figure out where it ended.

She found old fence posts and apple trees and wondered how they got there. Another mystery was an old abandoned coal mine on the edge of the hill. The entrance had been closed a long time ago so no one could get into it.

Along the woods and field, there were bits of barbed fence wire on several old posts. Who had lived around here and where did they go and why?

When rainstorms blew in during the summer, the creek would become a wild frenzy of rushing brown waters, spilling over its banks in the woods and sometimes spreading over their front yard not far from the house.

The water looked fierce and frightening, and she felt in awe of its mighty power. It was always a worry that they might get totally flooded.

In the winter she strapped ice skates on her shoes and skated on the frozen creek, pretending it was a canal in Holland, and that she was a famous ice skater. She also took her wooden skis and sled and soared over the frozen crest in the new fallen snow on the little hill.

Sometimes her dog, Princey, would bound along with her, trying to keep up with the skis or sled. One time Princey was running so fast that he couldn't stop himself in time, and crashed into the old shed at the foot of the hill!

Chapter 5

The Playhouse

Brigitta's father built a playhouse for her that was her pride and joy. It had red shingles just like the main house with real glass windows with screens to keep out the bugs. There was a screen door on the front door with a red awning over the doorway. Her mother wallpapered the inside so that the little house seemed not unlike the big house except for the size.

Tucked away in the valley between the mountains, she spent many days in the playhouse, pretending it was a school, hospital, or just a plain house, depending upon the cooperation of her dolls and teddybears.

In late June, Brigitta captured fireflies and put them in jars, setting them in the playhouse and watched as they cast shadows on the walls. Sometimes she brought in crayfish from the creek. She tried to remember to dump them back in the creek at night time but sometimes forgot, and felt bad when she saw their sad dead pitiful forms the next day.

One of Brigitta's favorite items in the playhouse was a rug with a design from India. When the sun shone through the windows, the dark colors sparkled and shone, reminding her of some far-off mysterious land.

Someday, she thought, she would like to travel there, but for now contented herself with the beautiful rug as well as the thick history books that her father let her browse through.

The playhouse was north of the big house, on the edge of the garden. In back of the garden was a wide field leading up to the hill that was called the "little hill." A bigger hill towered in back of the little hill.

Little Christmas trees dotted the little hill. She and her father had planted them when she was six years old.

All kinds of huckleberry bushes grew on the hills. On the 4th of July each summer, she and her mother would climb the hill with their pails and look for the first ripe blue huckleberries. One cup of berries was enough to make the thin pancakes that her mother made, serving them rolled up and sprinkled with sugar.

Huckleberry Pancakes

1 cup huckleberries

1 cup flour

1 egg

1 cup milk (more or less. Batter should be thin)

1 teaspoon sugar

Mix all ingredients well. Heat griddle. Brush griddle with shortening, making sure pan is not too hot or grease will splatter. Pour several spoonfulls of batter on hot griddle. Batter will be thin. Turn when pancakes start to brown.

Serve with sugar or jelly.

*or blueberries

Picking Berries on the Big Hill

The bad part about living down in the valley was the abundance of snakes. Garter snakes, she was told, were safe to be around, but rattlesnakes were a different matter. She was told to leave an area if she heard a rattle, as rattlesnakes were poisonous.

Sometimes she would find a garter snake curled up in a corner of her playhouse. Once in awhile when she was on the hill, she would find the dried out skin from a rattlesnake. Her father taught her not to be afraid, but to be watchful.

When Brigitta went walking through the wet fields or on the dry hill, she was always on the alert for snakes. If she found a garter snake in her playhouse she knew not to be afraid, but she hated the big water spiders that she would find clinging to the wallpapered walls. They were so hairy and awful looking.

Despite snakes and spiders, she loved living in the valley. She loved the smell of the meadow full of blue Quaker Ladies in the spring, and the smell of hickory nuts and hazelnuts in the fall. Brigitta loved the way the snow drifted down in the winter, covering the fir trees and meadows, making everything sparkly and white. No, she couldn't imagine living anywhere else.

Chapter 6

Dancing School

Suddenly it was time to take the annual school health exams. Brigitta dreaded the exams and was not too happy when the school nurse sent a note home with her stating that she was underweight for her age. She debated ripping up the note so as not to worry her mother. She knew her mother had enough things to worry about without worrying about her, too.

Brigitta's mother had to get up early every morning to go out to the barn to milk the cow. Then there was the job of straining milk each morning and evening, which meant spooning the cream from the rest of the milk. Brigitta's mother had many other chores, as well.

Reluctantly she gave the note to her mother, and was surprised later in the day when her mother suggested that maybe if she went to dancing school, she might gain some weight. Brigitta wasn't sure how that would help, but she was all for the idea.

That Saturday she and her mother went to visit Mary's School of Dance downtown in Clearfield, the little town that was across the Susquehanna River, three miles from their home.

The dance studio was in a building that housed the Ritz Theatre on one side and a restaurant on the other. The entrance to the studio was a long steep staircase leading to a door that opened into a very large room with shiny oak floors.

The walls were lined with tall oak chairs while two long narrow massive tables stood at the far end of the room by a row of high narrow windows.

The opposite end of the room had two doorways that led into two smaller rooms, one of which was used as a cloak room for coats and shoes and the other was the changing room to change clothes for classes. The practice room had a shiny pine wood floor with a new wood smell that made Brigitta feel at home. She knew she would like it right away.

Her mother enrolled her in acrobatic class and tap dancing class. Then they were off to shop for black patent leather shoes that tied in the front with a big black bow. She watched as the shoemaker put taps on the bottoms. She liked the click clack sound they made when she put them on.

She thought of the day this past summer when she and her mother had visited Mrs. Berry who lived a mile down the road from them in a very beautiful house on a hill. Mrs. Berry had a houseful of company. They were entertained by a little girl with long dark ringlets who, although blind, was able to tap dance while a lady played the piano.

Brigitta was fascinated and wondered how she did it, especially when she heard someone say that the little girl was also deaf.

Now she, too, would be able to tap dance, and she thought how wonderful that would be.

Acrobatic class was difficult. Because she was thin, it seemed that every bone in her body made contact with those hard shiny wood floors when she tumbled and rolled while doing summersaults and cartwheels.

Brigitta did not like the leg stretches, as they left her feeling stiff and sore. The dance instructor, Miss Bette, would walk down the row of girls lined up on the floor, and would push and stretch each leg, one at a time, to see how high they could go. Oh, how that hurt! She thought for sure her legs would break.

She was glad the acrobatic class was in the morning so she could get it over with. Tap class was later in the afternoon. Her mother had given her a quarter for lunch, so she went down to the restaurant in between classes. She was supposed to buy a sandwich for lunch, but mostly she couldn't resist the marshmallow sundaes. Often that's all she ate for lunch.

One Saturday when she went back to class earlier than usual, she was spellbound by what she saw. Students were lined up at a bar that stretched along one of the long walls and were performing the most graceful, beautiful motions that she had ever seen. She found out this was ballet class, and she knew right away that she just had to be in it.

When she asked her mother that night about the ballet class, her father insisted they would go broke if he had to pay for any more dance classes! But she pleaded and pleaded. She would even give up acrobatic class if she could take ballet. Eventually her mother gave in, but she wouldn't let her give up acrobatic class. She was stuck!

Dancing school became the most important part of her life. Suddenly she had something wonderful to participate in along with other girls some of whom were her own age. She had something else to think about.

Dancing school proved to be a whole different world from what she had known. It was a world of beautiful music, grace, soft leather acrobatic shoes, black shiny tap shoes, and now soft leather ballet slippers. Every Saturday meant attending dancing school. Brigitta loved it.

Since her father had to work on Saturdays, he was unable to drive her to dancing school. They only had one vehicle and, anyway, her mother didn't know how to drive. Brigitta's mother stood with her by the main road, and together they would hitch-hike a ride from people passing through on their way to town. Not many people drove on the main road, and her mother knew most of those who did. They never rode with people they did not know.

Sometimes her mother rode along with her into town unless she knew the person who had stopped for them. In that case, she would allow Brigitta to go to town without her.

Since dancing school classes lasted all day, Brigitta had no idea how her mother got back home on the days she rode with her, unless she walked the three miles. At the end of the afternoon, her parents would come for her as, like everyone else, they did their grocery shopping in town on Saturdays.

Brigitta would have time in between classes to go downtown where she would visit the 5 & 10-cent stores. There were two of them in Clearfield. One was at one end of the main street and the other one was at the other end. Both stores had wooden floors that creaked when walked on. Almost everything in the stores cost a nickel or dime, or at least was under a dollar.

Brigitta never had much money to spend, and she hated to ask her father for any since he was spending so much money sending her to dancing school.

Sometimes she spent her quarter on a movie instead of a sundae since the movie theatre was right beside the dance studio. In fact, when she climbed the stairs to get to the dance studio, the opposite door led to the movie theatre. When the door was open, she could peek in and watch the man running the movie projector. It seemed quite mysterious.

Making friends was a big part of dance school. Two of her best friends were twins, Louise and Louine. They were a year younger than her and wore their hair in long ringlets like she did. When they walked arm in arm downtown together, people thought they were triplets.

Dancing school was a whole new world. It made Brigitta feel

important, like she was someone famous and maybe, just maybe, she might be a famous dancer some day. She felt exceedingly happy, and when she went home, filled up her scrapbooks with pictures of famous ballerinas, other dancers, and movie stars.

Chapter 7

Realization

It was at school, of course, where she realized that she wasn't as pretty as some of the other girls. It was a quiet and saddening realization. How could some girls have such perfect features while she should be left out?

Although no one said anything about it, it was a known fact that her older sister, Mary, was the pretty one in the family. No, she found herself on the outside, as far as looks were concerned. Even her dentist said, "it must be hard having such a beautiful sister."

Her mother sewed princess-style dresses for her, but when you want to be pretty, and you're not, it's a painful feeling. Here you are, beginning life in the Big World, and finding out that LOOKS matter, and you don't have any. Woe!

Well, what did it matter after all. She decided she would be a famous ballet dancer, and imagined living in a big city and returning to Plymptonville wearing a red sweeping velvet cape. Yes, that's what she would do.

Dancing school absorbed her life. She would lose herself in the music, in the daily exercises of stretching and learning new steps. Each Saturday she became more and more limber until she found that it didn't hurt at all when she did the leg stretches.

She idolized the older dancers and knew that someday she would be like them. Meanwhile, she practiced and practiced.

The dresses that her mother made for her were special. Her mother could make something pretty out of anything, even a feed sack that had contained chicken feed. She often went to the feed store with her father and picked out a sack of feed that she thought had the best and prettiest design on it.

Once in a while she went with her parents to a little town thirty miles away where they could shop in special clothing stores that had a good selection of clothing. On one of those visits Brigitta chose a pale green suit with rhinestones on the lapel. She felt like a princess when she was able to walk out of the store with the treasured suit wrapped in a box, carefully hugged under her arm.

She couldn't do a thing about not being pretty. If you aren't, you aren't. Other things in the world were more important, or so she decided. At least she was able to grow up in a little valley that seemed like the most beautiful place in the world. She was glad she didn't have to live in town.

She loved the way the wind blew and howled through the trees in the woods just outside her bedroom. Sometimes the wind blew so hard that the windows would rattle and rattle. Her mother would stuff rags in them to stop the rattling, but Brigitta didn't mind the noise. She knew she was in a warm and safe house.

She also loved the mystery of the abandoned road that at one time had been built by the county. It seemed to go nowhere. She wondered what had been its purpose.

There was also a mystery about the big hill that towered over the little hill. Who used to walk on it before she came along? She loved to smell the pink wild roses that grew along the mountainsides and loved to hear the whip-poor-will singing his happy song from the top of a pine tree.

The little bungalow was cozy and warm. Her father would stoke the furnace with coal. Sometimes the furnace got so hot that it glowed fire red in the floor register and looked like a fiery monster. It scared her when it was that red but the heat felt good.

Her father was always adding on another room or porch to their house. Her mother kept it spotless by hanging fresh wallpaper every spring, painting walls, sewing curtains, and making braided rugs. It was necessary to put up fresh paint or wallpaper every spring due to the dust from the coal furnace.

Her mother was always baking bread or donuts, and on Saturday nights she often made chocolate cake with white whipped seven-minute frosting.

Studying to be a ballerina

23

Chapter 8

Things to Do

Even though Brigitta missed not having playmates close by, she loved living down in the valley. It was a quiet place and yet there was always something new and interesting to see every season. Along with huckleberries there were also luscious big blackberries that grew in big bushes up on the Big Hill.

She and her mother would get up early in the morning, put on long sleeved shirts and long pants, and head up the hill with their buckets. The heavy clothes they wore protected them from the hordes of mosquitoes as well as the sharp prickers on the berry bushes.

The blackberries ended up in pies or canned in jars for the winter. On their berry picking days, her mother would pack a basket with a jar of Kool-Aid to drink along with peanut butter sandwiches. The packages came with animal pictures in the inside.

Brigitta was collecting them and had quite a menagerie already of zebras, elephants and tigers.

The red fox lived up on the Big Hill. They often saw him watching with his bushy red tail and furry paws as he peered over a nearby log.

Gathering hickory nuts was a favorite activity in the fall. On those adventures her father would go with her and they would gather up nuts from the shagbark hickory nut trees that grew along the old abandoned county road.

Even though the nut shells were hard to crack and didn't contain a lot of meat, they still were tasty in cookies and fudge. Her mother used the nuts for her Christmas cookies.

Christmas Star Cookies

1. In a large bowl, cream 3/4 stick margarine, two well beaten eggs and 1 cup sugar

2. Add 3 cups flour, 1 teaspoon baking powder, 1/2 teaspoon salt and mix thoroughly

3. Add 1 teaspoon almond flavoring, 1 tablespoon milk and 1 teaspoon of grated lemon rind. Mix with wooden spoon. Add more or less flour until dough does not feel sticky or too thick.

4. Cover and chill overnight. Roll out and shape into stars. Sprinkle with a mixture of 1 medium well-beaten egg and 3/4 cup minced nuts with 1/4 cup sugar. Bake on ungreased cookie sheets for 8 to 10 minutes at 350 degrees. Cool and store.

Of all the places Brigitta liked to visit, the Big Hill was her very favorite place. She could take a book and curl up under a tree or just sit and listen to the whip-poor-will singing his happy songs.

Her mother was always busy milking the cow, baking bread or just taking care of the house, and didn't seem to worry about her. She could watch her from the big windows that faced the hill while she worked in the kitchen.

When Brigitta sat on top of the Big Hill, she could see smoke and hear the whoosh of several factories that stood far away on the other side of the Susquehanna River that separated the valley from the town. The "whoosh" was a comforting sound that she liked to hear as it echoed over the valley and mountain. Somehow or other it meant that things were all right in the world.

The "whoosh" noise came from the big tile factory, while big puffs of smoke curled from a huge sprawling brickyard factory that was close to the river. Every once in awhile she would hear the whistles from the big black steam engines that roared along the river near the brickyard. Most of the men who lived in the town and/or valley either worked in the brickyard, the tile factory or on the railroads that followed the Susquehanna River.

Chapter 9

The Little Bungalow

Red shingles covered the little bungalow that Brigitta lived in. It had two bedrooms and a small sitting room where her mother kept a treadle sewing machine. The sewing machine was under the window so her mother could look outside while she sewed. When her mother peddled the machine with her foot, it made a soft whirring sound.

There was a daybed in the sitting room that could be pulled out and made into a double bed when they had company. Aunts, uncles and cousins, it seemed, were always spending the night. That was because everyone lived so far away and it would be too late for them to start for home once it got dark.

The sitting room was where Brigitta kept her little table and chairs for her dolls when it was too cold in the winter to be in the playhouse. Her mother let her have real coffee in her cups along with sugar and milk which she served in little blue and pink teacups.

Brigitta shared her bedroom with Mary. Since her sister was six years older, they didn't seem to have a lot in common. Mary liked to keep her things scattered around. Brigitta had brown hair and brown eyes and liked to keep things neat.

Although they both slept in the same double bed, they kept an imaginary line across the room to keep things separated. They each had their own dresser but had to share the small closet.

The south window faced the woods and the west one faced the back yard.

The kitchen was quite large with a work table in the middle. A row of windows faced the north mountain. Her father was always adding something on to the house and was in the middle of building a breakfast nook on the east side of the kitchen.

Other rooms included her parents' bedroom and a new bathroom which her father had just built so they no longer had to go outside to the outhouse by the chicken coop.

Her father built a reservoir at the mountain edge and laid pipes from it to the house so they could have running water in the kitchen and the new bathroom. The bathroom faucets were shiny chrome with a red dot spigot for hot water and a blue dot spigot for cold water.

The living room floor was covered with linoleum and was where Brigitta practiced her dancing. The room was large and roomy with a bookcase on the east wall for all of her father's many books. Her mother's piano stood along another wall.

Between the living room and the kitchen was a hallway with a big floor register in the middle. In the winter Brigitta and her sister would spread their underclothing on the register so they would be warm and toasty before they got dressed to go outside. Under the register was a big coal furnace that glowed red when the coal in it was hot.

Brigitta would lie in bed in the mornings and could hear her father down in the basement stoking up the coal furnace. It would take awhile before the house got warm enough so she could get up.

On very cold winter mornings she could hear her father banging on the water pipes which might be frozen that meant there would be no running water until the pipes thawed out. The banging would help the ice to break up so the water could flow through the pipes.

Her father had dug a basement under the house for the furnace and for her mother's washing machine. Before that, her mother washed clothes on the back porch in a big galvanized tub with a scrub board. The tub was always getting holes in it and her mother had to patch the holes with a special cement.

In the basement there was also a little stove that was called "A Bucket a Day." That meant they had to keep putting coal in it all day long or they would not have any hot running water. Pipes from the little stove run up the ceiling and into the bathroom where they hooked into the pipes. Pipes also ran into the kitchen so there would be hot water, as well. If there wasn't any hot water in the faucets, that usually meant that either she or her sister had forgotten to feed the little stove with coal.

Chapter 10

Settlements Over the Mountain

On pleasant sunny summer days Brigitta and her mother visited some of the families who lived in little settlements over the mountains. They followed the old country road that wound past her bedroom on through the woods and on over the mountain.

Again, it was an abandoned road that had never been used except maybe by people many years ago on horseback or by carriage, winding over the mountain and leading into more widely-used dirt roads.

Several families lived back in the mountains along the dirt roads. Brigitta would walk over to visit these families that weren't too far away, but if she wanted to go further to visit other families, her mother came along.

A family with a lot of children lived in the closest mountain house. It was an old gray two-storied house way back along one of the dirt roads. Among the many children who lived there was a girl Brigitta's age. Her name was Peggy.

In the fall Brigitta liked to go to their house to watch them press apples in the big apple press. The whole back yard smelled like apples. Trampled-on crunched apples would be all over the ground. She couldn't help trampling on them while watching as everyone took turns churning the big press.

Peggy was very shy but once in a while would come over to visit Brigitta. They both liked to play with paper dolls.

Two other families lived further over the mountains. They, too, had big families. One of the families converted an old chicken coop into a playhouse. Brigitta loved to visit them and play in it. All the families seemed to be happy. Sometimes she would be invited to stay for dinner that was served around a big round table. When dinner was ready, everyone dipped their cups into the big soup bowl on the table to help themselves.

The mountain road at one place forked into two different directions; one led to town which was several miles away, and another led to a peaceful little farming community in the opposite direction, leading to an area called Mt. Joy.

Brigitta and her mother called the road "Skunk Hollow" because the woods along the road was full of skunk cabbage, a big green cabbage-like plant that grew in swampy areas. A tramp lived in the woods along the road, and although he seemed harmless, Brigitta was always careful to start running fast when she got close to the shack that he lived in.

Mt. Joy contained a number of sprawling farms that looked so pretty they didn't even seem real. The whole area was full of wide sprawling wheat fields, cows, fences, corn and meadows. A church with a white steeple stood beside a small graveyard. Another building close by served as a one-room school building.

Another direction led to town and past a hill where four houses stood. Brigitta was told that her parents rented one of the houses and that was where she was born during a cold blizzard on a January day.

The mountaintop was sunny and dry. She wondered why her family had chosen to live down in the valley instead of staying on the sunny mountain, but it was probably because there was no land available on the mountain for her father to buy and build on.

She loved to go hiking with her mother over the hill to visit some of the people in the four houses. In one of the four houses lived a lady, Mrs. Brown. She kept a doll in a little cradle in the living room. The doll looked just like a real baby. Brigitta knew she was not allowed to touch it. Brigitta felt sad for Mrs. Brown that she had no children of her own.

Brigitta sat quietly while her mother visited with her lady friends, even though it was hard to do so. She wondered what was upstairs or in the other rooms, but she didn't dare explore. She knew her mother probably got lonely being down in the valley with no neighbors in sight, and needed time to visit.

After tea and cookies, Brigitta and her mother started on their way home. They never dared to stay too long while visiting because dark shadows fell early in the mountains and they wanted to get home before dusk settled in.

They had to get home in time to fix supper for Brigitta's father, and also to milk the cow and feed the chickens. The cow would bawl and bawl if they were late for milking, and the chickens would squawk up quite a fuss if they didn't get their grain on time.

The path home led through patches of tea berries and wild brush. They had to step carefully to avoid getting scratched or even bitten by snakes that might be curled up among the rocks along the dirt road.

Chapter 11

Other Country Roads

The valley held other roads that were interesting, too. Brigitta's house was at the end of a long winding road that started at the main or paved road. She had to walk the main road for a mile to get to the bus stop to catch the school bus that took her to Plymptonville School.

The road to the bus stop wound over, up and down a hill that passed several fields and meadows before it came to a few houses. Brigitta often wondered what used to be along the road in the bare areas where a lilac bush bloomed or an apple tree stood here and there. Who used to live there at one time and what happened to them? She often had thoughts like that while she walked to keep herself from not being too lonely.

Not many cars went up and down the road, so it was a lonely walk. The settlement at the bus stop had a gas station and a big farm across the street and along the river. Once in a while she would go with her parents to the farm to visit while parties were being held. Brigitta especially liked the strawberry festivals.

A few years earlier, a one-room schoolhouse stood not too far from the farmhouse. Brigitta's sister attended the school for one year before it was torn down.

The people who owned the gas station were very friendly and

helpful. Brigitta knew that if she had a problem of some sort, she could go to them for help. The gas station's owners, Mr. and Mrs. Eberling, also raised Persian cats and sold kittens. One day when their cat had kittens, one was born with a club foot which meant the foot was bent in a crooked way. They offered to give the kitty to Brigitta, and she was happy to get it. The kitten, Fluffy, was cinnamon color with long fur.

The gas station store sold cream rolls filled with yummy Bavarian cream. Sometimes Brigitta's father stopped there on his way home from work to bring some home. On some summer days he also brought home ice cream cones that were wrapped in waxed paper so they would not melt before he got home.

A road wound past the gas station up a steep mountain to green rolling meadow hills and several beautiful farms. A school teacher, Mr. Fulton, lived on top of the hill in a big house with a wrap-around porch that overlooked the Susquehanna River as well as a train tunnel.

Brigitta liked to sit on their front porch where one could see not only the river but also some of the factories on the other side. It was quite a view. She especially liked to watch the steam locomotive trains that would puff in and out of the tunnel.

One summer she went with her family to attend a birthday party held in the Fulton's back yard. It was a large party with a big birthday cake and lots of pink lemonade.

Back down the mountain was the house where Mrs. Berry lived and where Brigitta had watched the little girl dance. Mrs. Berry was divorced and lived there with her small son, Bobby. Her house seemed fancier than Brigitta' s, with everything in its place. A stack of romance magazines were on the coffee table. Mrs. Berry had been married to a prosperous owner of a coal mine.

Once in a while Brigitta was asked to babysit for Bobby, and noticed that Bobby seemed to get anything and everything that he wanted, including a lunch box full of candy and pop. It never seemed to contain a sandwich.

Across from Mrs. Berry was a bungalow that sat along a mountain creek called Wolf Run. Brigitta and her Mother visited a lady, Helen, who lived there with her husband and a young child that slept in a cradle in the hallway. The child could not sit up, talk, or walk, even though she was about Brigitta's age.

On the wall above the cradle was a large brown cabinet that held a black telephone. When it rang five rings, Helen answered it. Every family that had a telephone in their house had a different ring.

There was a crank on the telephone that had to be wound before the telephone could be used. Brigitta's family did not yet have a telephone, so she thought it was quite the marvelous invention.

A little dog, Tippy, was down in the basement. When Brigitta went downstairs to visit the dog, it jumped on her and bit her finger. She never trusted little dogs again.

Birthday party on the mountain

Chapter 12

Neighboring Farmhouses

There were no other houses along the paved road that led back to Brigitta's house except for the Burnsworth farm way across the fields along the road, and also the sprawling Zempka farm on top of the hill in another direction. The beautiful Breth house was hidden in the woods high on the mountain overlooking the Susquehanna River.

Mr. Breth was an important person in the town and was well liked by everyone. Brigitta and her parents knew the people in all of those houses and visited them from time to time.

The Burnsworth farm contained a large two-story white house, a big red barn, lots of out buildings and lots of cows, including a big black bull. The house had a big front porch with a large doorway that opened up to a hallway with a winding circular stairway leading upstairs.

To the left of the stairway was the biggest dining room Brigitta had ever seen. She visited the daughter, Ruthie, who lived there. Ruthie's Mother had died recently so it as up to Ruthie to do the kitchen and laundry work for her father.

In the dining room was a big white machine that Ruthie used for pressing clothes. Some days Brigitta and Ruthie played Monopoly on the big dining room table.

The large living room was on the other side of the winding stairway. It seemed, to Brigitta, too big to be cozy since the chairs and sofa were so far apart.

The kitchen was huge! A collection of pots and pans hung from the ceiling above a long work table. There was a big kitchen table and rows and rows of cupboards. Tall narrow windows lined one of the walls. It was a cream-colored kitchen, nice and airy.

One of the doors in the kitchen led to a huge room, like a big garage, where milk was brought in from the cows to be strained and put into milk cans. Along one wall was a row of stainless steel sinks and tubs where various equipment was washed. This was the area where the milk from the cows was brought in, separated and prepared to be delivered into town. The floor was bare cement and very clean. Someone was always washing it down with a hose.

A staircase off the kitchen led to the upstairs. There was a large balcony/porch off one of the upstairs rooms. That's where Ruthie hung the laundry when it was raining outside.

Besides a number of bedrooms upstairs, there was another staircase that led to a third level of rooms that were sometimes rented out. Brigitta heard that before her father built their little house in the valley, they rented some of the rooms. Sometimes the renters had small children, and Brigitta would be asked to babysit. She liked to sit with the little children. She enjoyed playing games and victrola music for them.

One of the children had the largest collection of records of stories and songs she had ever seen. She would spend the evening playing the records over and over until whomever she was babysitting fell fast asleep.

When Brigitta was done babysitting, the parents would drive her home down the long winding road to the little bungalow.

Outside in the backyard, a swing hung from the huge maple tree where Brigitta could swing so high that it seemed she was soaring over the grapevines that grew along the edge of the yard.

The hillside behind the white farmhouse held huckleberry bushes that grew everywhere. The berries that ripened in July grew on bushes close to the ground. They were small but sweet berries. Larger berries grew on taller bushes that bloomed in early August.

There were so many berries that buckets and tubs could be filled quickly. Some of the berries were taken to town where they were sold and sent off to the big cities.

Brigitta's mother canned a lot of berries. They tasted so good in the middle of the winter. She would serve them in a dessert dish or use them for pies and other desserts.

Huckleberry Crumble Dessert

3/4 cup flour

4 cups huckleberries or blueberries

1 cup brown sugar

3/4 cup uncooked oatmeal

1/2 cup butter, melted

1 teaspoon vanilla

Preheat oven to 350 degrees.

Spread berries on bottom of a two-quart baking dish or pan. Mix flour, sugar, oatmeal, butter and vanilla and spread over berries. Bake 45 minutes.

Serve warm. The cake is especially good with ice cream.

A huge red barn stood along the highway beside the big white farm house. It housed many cows and a very big black bull that sometimes would be left to graze in the field across the main highway. Brigitta was afraid of the bull and stayed close to her house when it was outside.

Brigitta remembered when Ruthie's mother was alive and how she served marshmallows and apples during Halloween. The big house seemed very quiet and lonely without her.

Chapter 13

Playmates

There were few children to play with down in the valley. Brigitta was happy when the third floor of the big white farmhouse was rented out to a family that had a little girl, Marion, her own age.

Marion was little and pudgy, and sometimes went into a trance when she would suddenly stand still and stare straight ahead. Her mother said that was due to a health problem.

One day they were both walking on the main road to catch the school bus when Marion went into a trance in the middle of the road. Brigitta quickly pushed her out of the way just as a car came whizzing by.

Marion had a big collection of expensive dolls that she was not allowed to play with. They were all lined up in a big glass cabinet and seemed to stare as if they were as lonesome as Brigitta felt sometimes. Brigitta didn't think that was fair to Marion or to the dolls. She was glad that she was allowed to play with her own dolls and didn't have to keep them in a glass cupboard or boxes.

But Marion and her parents didn't stay long in their apartment. One day they packed up and moved to another town. Brigitta missed her when she moved away.

Because there seldom was anyone her age to play with, she took great comfort in having her dolls and playhouse. She could sit in the playhouse and pretend that she was in India or some other far-away place.

The sun would shine through the windows and beam down on the tapestry rug that her mother had allowed her to have in the playhouse. Brigitta would close her eyes and pretend she was far away.

There weren't many children who lived with the friends she and her parents visited. When there was someone her age, it seemed that they always hid behind the curtains or their mother's apron. Maybe they were shy because they, too, were lonely and didn't know how to greet strangers like herself.

School and dancing school was where she could visit with children her own age. She also liked to visit the library that was around the corner from the dancing school. There she found many wonderful books, including the Louisa Alcott series of "Little Women."

In the evening, Brigitta and her father would both curl up in the big chair and read books together. Her father would order books through the mail. Some of the books had great pictures and stories of far-away lands.

Having a good book to read made up for not having a friend to play with. She could transport herself to another world while reading a good book.

While she and her father curled up with books, her mother would play the piano. Her mother was a great pianist and could play almost anything. The music would seem to drift through the house and drown out the wind that might be blowing against the shingles on cold winter nights.

Chapter 14

Coal Mining Towns

Almost every Sunday Brigitta and her parents drove to two little mining towns in the mountains where her great aunts and uncles lived. Her Tante Krause (Aunt Krause) and Uncle Krause lived in an old two-story gray wooden building.

The rooms inside were dark and the furniture was mostly dark, as well, with big wooden arms on the chairs and sofa. The floors were wooden and bare but a cozy stove was in the center, and in the cold weather the warmth from the stove felt good.

Tante and Uncle Krause were always happy to greet them. Tante Krause had sponsored her father to come from Germany. That meant she had sent him money to pay for the ticket to travel on the big ocean liner. She always served them warm kuchen, a yummy cake topped with brown sugar and cinnamon and made sure to send some home with them, as well.

Brigitta would sit and listen to them chatter away in German. They talked so fast that she couldn't understand much of what was said. She spent a lot of time imagining what might be upstairs or in some of the other rooms but she didn't dare go to inspect them. Instead she looked longingly at a kewpie doll that stood on a shelf in the living room bookcase. She never did get to play with the kewpie doll but instead was given warm milk to drink and pieces of warm kuchen.

Visiting Tante Krause

Uncle Krause kept goats, chickens and ducks, and was always busy taking care of them. Brigitta suspected that the warm milk she was given was goat milk. She didn't really care for goat milk!

At the end of summer Tante Krause dug up petunias and put them in little pots that she set around the windows in the living room. Brigitta liked their sweet smell.

Brigitta felt that Tante Krause must be unhappy as her voice sounded angry when she talked about her children who had moved far away. Although Brigitta couldn't understand all that was said, it sounded like their two sons didn't visit very often, and she felt sad as she watched Tante Krause twisting and wringing a handkerchief in her hands while she talked.

Brigitta knew her father was only nineteen when he came over from Germany. She wondered what Germany looked like, and how hard it must have been for him to leave his mother and father to come to a strange land.

Another aunt and uncle lived just a mile down the road in the same area. Brigitta knew the two couples, for some reason, did not get along with each other and did not visit. They seemed like two lonely couples who lived far away from their homeland and families, and she wondered what made them leave their homeland.

The towns where the two couples lived were coal mining towns with tall towering tipples that led into the dark dreary coal tunnels. Beside the mines stood huge piles of discarded coal called boney piles that seemed always to be on fire with an awful smell that drifted far over the mountains. The smell was so bad that you could smell it for miles. Most of the men who lived in the towns worked in the mines.

Orange sulfur sometimes seeped out of the mines and drifted into the little mountain streams, turning them a smelly orange color. No one seemed to mind the smell of the air or the orange of the water, since everyone worked in the mines and didn't know how to fix either one of those problems. They were just grateful for the jobs the mines provided.

Brigitta's grandmother also lived in one of the little towns. Her gray two-story house was on top of a hill with a long winding driveway. Brigitta hid in the back seat of the car every time they drove up the narrow road. She was always fearful they would crash into another car coming down while they were driving up.

Tante Krause planting flowers

Chapter 15

Grandmother's House

Brigitta liked visiting Grandmother Lipka, the only grandmother she knew, since her other grandparents lived in Germany and she never got to meet them. Grandfather Lipka had died a few years ago from a mining accident. Someone said he died after falling on a pick used in the mines. The injury somehow or other caused a condition that poisoned his blood.

Brigitta heard many stories about her grandfather and how he would wake up the children by blowing his big trombone in the mornings. He sounded like a nice grandpa but now he was buried in the little family cemetery just over the hill, walking distance from the house.

Grandma married again soon after grandfather's death as she was left alone with eight children to raise and had no money. There were no pensions for widowed women. Grandpa Augustine, the man who was chosen for grandma to marry was not, or so Brigitta thought, very friendly. In fact, she thought of him as a grumpy man.

Brigitta heard that he had left a family in Illinois. She didn't know if his first wife had died or what happened to the children, so that he could marry her grandmother. He didn't seem very happy about it all. Maybe he regretted taking on a second family with so many children.

There was a big ornate pump organ in grandmother's living room. No one seemed to know how to play it as Brigitta never heard it being played. The big house seemed to be drafty and cold but there always seemed to be a big pot of potatoes boiling on the black iron stove in the kitchen. Grandma always had a nice dinner for them.

Grandma Lipka was her mother's mother. Brigitta's mother and father had been married in this house when a big snowstorm had prevented them from being married in the little German Lutheran St. Paul Church by the cemetery.

The front door that led to the living room had a glass window in it with the carving of a deer. Brigitta thought it was quite beautiful.

All of the beds in the house were covered with big soft feather bed comforters. She wished she had one of those on her own bed.

Just off the kitchen was a little room with a hand pump on a counter for water. A big gray tub used for taking baths or washing clothes hung on the wall of the little room. It all seemed very clean and cozy.

Outside was a gray barn and several apple trees that in the fall had delicious yellow apples. Brigitta liked to climb the trees.

One day while they were visiting, she heard her grandmother talk about possibly moving to Illinois. It seemed that Grandpa Augustine was thinking of taking a job there and wanted them to move.

Brigitta knew she would miss them and the big old house, even though it seemed the house always smelled of Ben Gay that grandma used to ease the pain of sore muscles.

On the way home they drove over to the little cemetery where Grandpa Lipka was buried. The cemetery was on top of a hill in back of the German Lutheran St. Paul Church, a gray wooden church building where Grandma and Grandpa Lipka had both taught Sunday School. Grandpa Lipka had also been the choir master.

Several concrete steps led up to the church. The door was unlocked. Brigitta walked through the doorway and gazed up at the choir loft. She tried to imagine her grandfather being up there and leading the singing.

The building was empty now and no longer used. A wooden podium was at the front of the church. She could imagine a pastor standing there and talking in German. Only birds sang in there now as they flew in and out of a broken window.

Grandfather Lipka was buried in the little cemetery in back where forget-me-nots bloomed on his grave. Across from his grave was the grave of her uncle, Johann, who died when he was just two years old.

Grandmother Lipka

Chapter 16

Trips to Coalport

One of Brigitta's mother's sisters, Aunt Martha, lived in Coalport. Coalport was another little mining town. Uncle Bill worked in the mine, as did most of the men in town.

It took more than an hour to drive to Coalport and sometimes Brigitta or her sister, Mary, would get carsick from the bumpy roads. They took comic books to read along the way to try to keep their minds occupied, as well as a bucket just in case they got sick.

If they went to Coalport over Easter time, Brigitta took her Easter basket, but more than once when the sun shone in the back car windows, the chocolate bunnies and eggs would be melted by the time they got there.

The roads were too slippery and icy in the wintertime to go on long trips, so they drove to Coalport only when the weather was nice. Winter meant Brigitta's father had to put chains on the car tires. At times a chain would break and would make a "click click clickety" sound. Then they had to pull over while Brigitta's father fixed the chain. That was not a pleasant job to do which was why they avoided going to Coalport in the winter.

Aunt Martha kept a spotless house. She was always sweeping and dusting. It was a bigger and fancier house than Brigitta's. Brigitta loved visiting Aunt Martha and Uncle Bill. Uncle Bill would take her shopping downtown and let her pick out special things. Uncle Bill was a tall slender and kind man. He always made her feel very special.

Uncle Bill always took off his shoes when he entered the house. Brigitta's father scoffed at that and said, "A man ought to be able to wear shoes in his own house."

Sometimes she would spend the night. But one time she got homesick and they had to drive her all the way back to Wolf Run to take her home to the little bungalow.

Aunt Martha dressed very plain and wore her hair in a bun whereas Brigitta's mother had curly hair from permanents.

The house was stucco on the outside and had a big front porch with white snowball bushes growing around it. Aunt Martha was just as fussy about the yard as she was about the house. In fact, several times when they visited, she asked Brigitta to pull out the lanky Buckhorn plantain in the yard. Brigitta didn't mind doing that although she secretly thought it was Aunt Martha's way to keep her out of the spotless house.

Aunt Martha had two grown children, Marie and Billy. Billy had joined the United States Army. One Christmas he sent Brigitta a package. When she opened it, she saw a beautiful doll with blue glass eyes that opened and closed. The doll was dressed in a white organdy dress. Brigitta called the doll "Priscilla."

Marie liked to sew and one day made a blue and white polka- dotted dress for Priscilla.

Aunt Martha had the newest and most expensive furniture in her house. She even had an electric sewing machine.

Chapter 17

Electricity Comes to the Valley

Although Brigitta loved to visit her aunts and uncles, she loved the little Wolf Run bungalow that seemed cozy and warm with love and happiness.

Shiny kerosene lamps were lit at night time. Her family had to be careful around the lamps so that they didn't get knocked over. One night one of the lamps did get tipped over and set fire to Brigitta's father's favorite chair. The fire was quickly put out but the chair was never the same after that, even though her mother put a cover over it.

Although the lamps gave out a warm cozy glow, no one stayed up late at night and, instead, went to bed early. All of that changed one day when a big truck pulled into their yard and a man came to the door telling them that they would be putting up poles for electric lines. This meant they would finally have electricity and would no longer use the kerosene lamps.

Brigitta watched as the men put up eight tall utility poles along their long winding driveway. She didn't much like the poles and the wires they strung on them as they seemed to ruin the lovely countryside view. Each pole cost four dollars. Her father said that was a lot of money just for poles.

Soon the little bungalow in the valley was full of wires and plugs that looked ugly and got in the way. Electricity changed the way of life for everyone. Now, with electric lights all over the house, Brigitta's family could stay up late to listen to the big wooden radio that her father brought home one day.

They all enjoyed listening to the radio. One of Brigitta's favorite programs was "Henry Aldridge." Her father liked "Just Plain Bill, while her mother preferred "Stella Dallas."

One day when Aunt Martha and Uncle Bill brought her home to the valley after she had spent the night, no one was home, and they couldn't get in the house as the front door was locked. The door had never been locked before. They walked around the back of the house until they found a bedroom window they could push open. Uncle Bill lifted Brigitta up so she could slip through the window and open the front door.

As soon as they entered, Brigitta noticed that the house had a different feeling now that electricity had been installed. There was a strange smell of new appliances. Brigitta's parents had been busy shopping while she was away, and in the kitchen was a tall shiny white refrigerator that made a strange humming sound. No longer would Brigitta's mother have to put perishable foods by the creek to stay cool, only to lose them when flash floods from heavy rains occurred.

The big green kerosene stove had been replaced by a white electric range. Even the washtub and washboard had been replaced by an electric washing machine that had a wringer on the top to wring the water out of the laundry. Brigitta was glad the washboard had been replaced. Scrubbing clothes on it was hard on her knuckles.

The tin washtubs were placed on the back porch. They made perfect boats to ride in the creek. Brigitta almost drowned one day when her cousin playfully dumped her when she was in one of the tubs. The creek had deep spots and low spots. The spot she nearly drowned in was a very deep one. She was afraid to put the tubs in the water after that whenever her cousin was visiting.

In the summer, her father used the tubs on the back porch to take a bath in when he came home from the mines.

Chapter 18

Brigitta's Father

When her father came home in the evenings after working in the coal mines, he was totally black with coal dust. Because they had no neighbors, he was able to take a bath on the back porch where no one could see him, other than the cows and chickens!

Her father wore long underwear under his mining clothes as the mines were wet and damp. Her mother had to wash the clothes almost every evening. She hung them outside on the clothesline where in the winter they froze solid and looked like stiff headless people.

Every day when her father went to the mines, he wore a hard helmet with a small carbide lantern attached to it. The lantern contained a small well area for water. When carbide, a chemical, was poured into the well and a match was struck, there was just enough light to help the miners see what they were doing while deep in the mines.

Her father was a mine foreman and had to be at the mines before anyone else arrived. That meant he left very early in the morning to get to work and came home very late at night. He took sticks of dynamite with him to use for clearing out tunnels. He had to pay for the dynamite himself as the company he worked for did not pay for work supplies.

The dynamite was kept in a large wooden box marked with a big red X and kept in the garage. No one but Brigitta's father was allowed to touch the box as dynamite was highly explosive.

Working in the mines was very dangerous. Workers were injured or even killed when rocks fell, or if they were struck by the dynamite, or caught in a cave-in. It seemed that someone was always getting injured.

One day Brigitta was allowed to go down into the mine with her father so she could see what it was all about. The entrance to the mine looked like the opening to a cave that tunneled deep into the mountain. The opening they walked into was dark and spooky. The ceilings were low and the floor was wet. Water dripped from the ceiling. It did not seem a nice place to work. Rocks and boards lined the sides of the tunnel.

A railroad track ran down the middle of the tunnel so that coal could be moved on special carts out of the mine and up to the tipple just outside of the mine entrance.

The tipple was a high building structure that looked like a roller coaster that ended in mid-air. Miners shoveled coal onto the coal cars that were pushed up the tracks out of the mine to the tipple where the cars were dumped into trucks and/or regular railroad cars that took the coal to towns and cities.

Some of the cars were pushed up the tracks by the miners and some were pulled by big strong horses. Some of the cars had pulleys which the miners used to pull them out of the mine.

There was a series of rooms inside the mine, with rocky roofs supported by heavy wooden beams which, her father said, sometimes came down, injuring the miners. Gas was something the miners had to worry about, too. If the mine was not ventilated enough, an explosion might result from the coal gas.

Men grumbled about the hard work in the mines but since there were few other jobs available, they were glad to have the work. These were the years of the Big Depression when there were not enough jobs for people nor was there enough money for food for everyone. Some lawyers and even doctors had to work in the mines just to get enough money for food for their families.

Besides the carbide lamp, helmet, and dynamite, Brigitta's father also carried an iron pick that was used to loosen the coal. Brigitta looked at the big sweating horses pulling coal cars and thought they probably didn't like this kind of work either.

Brigitta's father got grouchy when he was home and sometimes yelled at her mother for no reason. He would complain that his Sunday shirt collar wasn't ironed right or that he couldn't find a letter that he wanted to read RIGHT NOW. He even complained about the lunch her mother packed for him.

Sometimes the whole family would be dressed to go to the movies and her father would get mad about something, so they couldn't go. Brigitta was sure it was all because of the unpleasant working conditions that he had to endure every day in the mines.

One day her mother got so upset from the complaining that she packed her suitcase and took off. But she came back after a little while. She didn't know how to drive a car so she couldn't go very far. Brigitta felt sorry for her mother and father as they both worked so hard and sometimes life just didn't seem fair. She was glad if company came to visit because then her parents would "make up" and things would get back to normal.

Brigitta thought a lot about her father's temper and decided the mines were to blame. Other than for his bouts of temper, Brigitta loved her father. She felt that both her mother and father were special the way they could speak German to each other and no one else knew what they were saying.

They both always dressed very nice. Her father always wore a topcoat, hat, scarf and gloves when he went to town, and looked quite handsome. He was a good-looking trim man with sky blue eyes and a head of wavy hair.

Her mother dressed sharp, too. She regularly went to the beauty parlor for permanents or to get her hair set. During the day she wore pretty house dresses, socks and heavy shoes. She never wore slacks. In the winter she wore a big fur coat that she carefully put in cold storage during the summer. They were a handsome pair, her parents, and Brigitta was proud of them.

The Coal Miners

Chapter 19

Farm Animals

One summer Brigitta's father brought home Bob, a work horse from the mine. "I'm saving him from the glue factory," he said. "That's where old horses go." The horse was a big chestnut brown horse. He looked strong and powerful even though he was old. When he stomped on the floor of the gray barn shed, it seemed the floor might give in. But it didn't.

Brigitta thought Bob had sad eyes. Certainly he had long eyelashes. She wondered if horses could think and, if so, what was he thinking? Was he glad to be out of the mines? She didn't try to ride Bob as he looked so big and scary that she stayed her distance. And yet his presence seemed comforting, as if something so big could keep everything safe around them.

One day Brigitta's father told her to stand on Bob's back while he took their picture. Although she was scared, she let her father put her on Bob's back. She had put on the new red and white bathing suit her father had just bought for her when he was in Camp Grayling for the National Guards. It felt scary to be so high off the ground but she was able to stand still long enough to have her picture taken.

Bob stayed with them for a year until the day she came home from her girlfriend's house and saw that he was gone. "Sold," said her father.

How could he sell him without telling her? She felt betrayed somehow.

Things changed all the time on the little farm. She tried not to get too friendly with the chickens because every time she named one it would end up in the stew pot. She did, however, enjoy watching the mother hens and their little baby chickens as they wandered all around the yard. If they wandered into the woods, that would be bad news as a skunk or fox would get them.

Then, one day, her father brought home a pig. He was a clean pig, as pigs go, and stayed in the fenced area behind the barn. He made funny squealing sounds when she tried to pet him. He was supposed to be bacon and ham eventually but he, too, disappeared one day. Her father said another farmer came along and bought him as he didn't have the heart to butcher him.

Even the cows were traded off for other cows from time to time, which was okay as some were friendly and some were not. Some used their horns to let people know just how they felt. The veterinarian came one day to dehorn one of them, but just as he reached over to do the job, the cow suspected something was up and tossed him across the field. Luckily, he was not hurt.

Cows were like that. They seemed to be stubborn and out-right cantankerous. It was Brigitta's job to use a fly sprayer to chase away the flies that bothered them. She didn't like that job as the cow didn't know what she was up to and sometimes would flip her tail around and give her a big smack!

They didn't use fences for their cows but instead used a long chain that was attached to a big iron stake. Brigitta's mother would move the stake here and there to different grazing grounds, and pound it into the ground so the cow couldn't run away.

One day the cow yanked the stake out and wandered away. They looked everywhere for it. Brigitta helped in the search and while walking over one of the hills, she encountered a big black bull that was standing in a field. Brigitta carefully walked around the outside of the field and hoped that the bull wouldn't jump the fence and attack her. Finally, a neighbor found the cow and brought her home.

Brigitta's mother was small and didn't have a lot of muscle for pounding stakes, but she did her best. Brigitta watched her pound the stakes and wondered how she was able to do it.

But for all the bother, the cows were worth it because Brigitta loved the fresh whipping cream her mother skimmed off the milk in the early mornings.

It was used to top the hot chocolate beverage that she drank with her toast every morning and was so delicious!

Chapter 20

Valentine's Day

All in all, the rest of the fourth year of school went well. Except for Valentine's Day, that is. Everyone was encouraged to make a Valentine's Box to place on their desks. Much work went into them, with red and some white construction paper along with tissue paper.

Brigitta liked working on the boxes as they all looked so pretty with their red hearts and lacy doilies. Soon everyone had a finished box and waited patiently for the distribution of cards.

Before the cards were distributed, Mrs. Winters served pink Kool-Aid and big fat pink frosted Valentine cookies. Brigitta was so anxious for the cards that she could hardly wait.

Everyone placed their cards in a large box on Mrs. Winter's desk. Ward and Mary were chosen to distribute them.

Into the boxes on everyone's desks, went the Valentines, one by one. Since it was a large class, it took a long time. The school was a consolidated school which meant that several smaller schools had closed and now those students were attending Brigitta's school. It had happened during the middle of winter and no one was happy to have to share their classrooms with a bunch of other students.

Once the other students arrived, the school seemed to be busier and more crowded than ever. It took some time for everyone to adjust to this new situation.

Some of the students came from a few small towns that no one thought much of, and some students who were bused in from communities down in the hollows were called names such as "Ridge Runner" or "Hillbilly." Even Brigitta was sometimes called a "Ridge Runner" since she lived out in the country, but after a while everyone started to get along with each other.

Finally, all of the cards were distributed. Everyone eagerly started sorting through them. Brigitta felt left out when she noticed that some of the prettier girls got cards that were especially frilly or fancy while she received plain ordinary ones.

"Well," she thought, "so much for Valentine's Day. I'll get even with everyone some day when they realize that I'm a famous ballet dancer!" That was her hope, anyway. She resolved to practice her dancing every day until she got really good. She would show them all!

Chapter 21

The Horrible Accident

Max would not be coming back to school! His sister, Ruby, was seriously injured! Everyone was stunned.

Max and Ruby lived in a dilapidated older house by the railroad tracks along the river on the outside of town. They were both very shy and had six brothers and sisters. Brigitta felt they were shy because they felt embarrassed for being poor. Now today the class was told that Max would not be back, ever, and that Ruby had lost a leg.

Mrs. Winters looked distraught as she told the class about the bad accident. Max and Ruby's father worked in the mines and kept a box of dynamite in a shed by their house.

For some unknown reason, the dynamite exploded, killing Max and injuring Ruby. The whole class was shocked. Brigitta thought of the box of dynamite marked with a red "X" in her father's garage and vowed to stay far away from it.

She looked over at Max's empty desk. She felt sorry for Ruby to lose a leg. Although Max and Ruby were a year apart in age, they were both in the same class because Max had been held back a year due to illness. He had been a small, thin boy, while Ruby was a big girl. Everyone bowed their heads while Mrs. Winters said a prayer for the family.

Brigitta wondered when Ruby would be able to return and how would she manage with just one leg?

Violence, it seemed was ever present. Men were injured or killed in the coal mines or even driving on their way to and from work when the mountains were covered in fog, and they couldn't see clearly to drive on the narrow winding roads.

There would be swimming accidents such as drowning when someone jumped off one of the many iron bridges over the wide Susquehanna River and got trapped in deep water. Brigitta thought of the several times she had nearly drowned in the little creek by her house.

One other time she nearly drowned when she went swimming with her girlfriends at a lake by their house. She had stepped off a board and down she went into water over her head and, for a while, she couldn't get herself out. It had scared her so much that after that she was extra careful not to go in water over her head.

There were accidents on some of the farms. Someone would have accidents with tractors, hay machines, or would fall into the big silos that held silage for the farm animals.

Some girls and/or mothers would get injured when their blouses or dresses got caught in the wringers on the big new electric washing machines. Or someone would be canoeing or fishing in the rivers and would upset and drown.

Chapter 22

World War II

When the World War II raged on, air raid drills were held in the schools. Brigitta's class was told to hide under their desks while shades were pulled down just in case the enemy sent airplane bombers over their town.

Everyone knew about the destruction that bombs could do, as every time they went to the theaters or movie houses, the newsreels showed the awful bombing that was happening all over Europe.

Stamps were sold to help "Uncle Sam." "Uncle Sam" was the name given to the United States to help fund the war efforts. Almost every student in Brigitta's room had a book used to paste stamps in.

Once the book was full, it was exchanged for a Savings Bond that was used to help purchase supplies and/or equipment for the men and women who served in the war.

In the fall students were asked to gather milkweed pods from plants that grew along the roads and bring them to school by the bushelful. The pods were used for many things, including life vests or parachutes for the soldiers.

Everything was affected by the war. Because so many supplies were needed to help the soldiers, there were shortages of food and gasoline.

Every family had a ration book which instructed them how much they were allowed to purchase. Brigitta's mother was allowed to buy only a small amount of sugar. It was never enough for the baking she liked to do.

Brigitta's mother took coats and/or other garments to exchange for a coupon for sugar with a large family that lived over the mountain and who needed clothing more than sugar.

Special coupons were given to each family for the purchase of gasoline for their automobiles. They were distributed according to the size of the family and how far the head of the family had to drive to get to work.

Brigitta's family was in the "limited driving" range which meant they were given only enough coupons to buy gas for her father to get to work and back. This limited the trips they could take to visit the aunts and uncles that lived in other towns.

Every family had someone involved in the war. Brigitta's father was too old to enlist or to be drafted so he joined the National Guard. He had to attend regular training sessions as well as Guard Camp during the summer.

Although Brigitta missed him when he was gone, she liked the postcards he would send to her. He also brought presents when he came home.

The National Guard Armory held regular dances that her family attended. Her mother and father both liked to dance. It was there where she learned how to polka dance when her father took her out on the floor and showed her the steps. She loved to do the polka with her father.

Almost every house had a banner in their windows or on their doors if a family member was involved in the war. The banners had either gold or silver stars depending upon whether their soldier was alive or dead. It was a time of great sadness for many people.

Brigitta was glad that she was able to bring milkweed pods to school or some money for savings bonds. When she went to the movies and watched all the newsreels, she thought she might like to be an army nurse or serve in the armed forces as a service woman. She liked the snappy uniforms they wore.

The newsreels at the movie theaters kept everyone informed on what was happening all over Europe. It all sounded and looked quite awful. Sometimes Brigitta would have nightmares about planes coming to bomb her home. She was always glad to wake up the next morning to realize that she was okay. People tried to be brave and patriotic.

Together they sang songs such as "Over here, over there," or "My Bonnie Lies Over the Ocean." The songs made everyone feel better.

Despite the hardships and scarcity of food, Brigitta watched as her mother and father wrapped up food goods and hid them in clothing to send to relatives in Germany. Many of the relatives were suffering from all the bombing and destruction. They were not followers of the evil dictator, Adolph Hitler, but had to remain quiet for their own safety. That's the way of war. There are good people and bad people.

Chapter 23

The Circus

After the World War II, people tried to find happiness wherever they could. When the circus came to town, which it did once a year, Brigitta and her classmates got quite excited. It would be in town only for one day and no one wanted to miss it. Posters announcing the circus were plastered everywhere. Sometimes the school would close for the day, but this year was not the case.

"I'm going anyway," said Mike. "My mother said it was ok with her." Soon there were whispers in little groups all over the playground, and Brigitta could just feel the excitement in the air. It seemed that quite a few students were going whether the school excused them or not.

"But how can you go?" asked Brigitta. "It will be an unexcused absence." They had just finished playing a game of "Annie come over," and she was standing next to Tom and Ellen. It was a warm May day. Summer was on its way. Going to the circus sounded like more fun than sitting in school.

"If your mother signs the slip, then it's okay," said Tom. Brigitta wondered if her mother would sign one. That night after supper was done Brigitta decided to be brave and ask her mother. "The circus is coming to town for just one day. A lot of my friends are going. Can I go, too? It will be on the fairgrounds down the valley from the school."

"Circus," said her sister as they all sat around the table finishing dessert of strawberry shortcake. "Why would you want to go? I think circuses are dumb." Brigitta glared at her sister but tried hard not to say anything. If they argued, she might lose any chance of going.

She decided to say, "Ellen is going and I could walk with her," hoping that might convince her mother.

"Well," said her mother. "If Ellen is going, then I suppose you can go. It would be a shame to miss it since it comes only once a year."

Brigitta was so happy she nearly jumped out of her seat. The day of the circus was sunny and warm. Brigitta walked over to Ellen's house for lunch, something she often did since Ellen lived so close to the school.

They both decided not to turn in their permission slips until the next day, just in case Mrs. Winters gave them a bad time. This gave a great sense of adventure to the whole experience, as without the slip they could be accused of "playing hooky."

On circus day Brigitta went to Ellen's house for lunch. From there they watched as everyone else filed back into the school.

Quietly and cautiously, they sneaked behind houses near the school so they wouldn't be seen. Down through the trees and into a dry ravine they slowly walked, pretending they were spies on a mission.

They could hear the circus music playing from the big tent and could see elephants standing solemnly nearby. Brigitta couldn't wait to get there. She knew she would see tigers and lions, too. What fun!

Finally, they reached the fairgrounds just as they heard the ticket man holler out for all to hear "Get your tickets here! This way! Get your tickets." They each handed him twenty-five cents. Brigitta's heart was pounding so fast she thought it would leap right out!

She and Ellen climbed over the wooden benches and found a seat. "Well now," thought Brigitta, "let the circus begin."

Chapter 24

Summer Vacation

May was one of Brigitta's favorite months. Birds were singing everywhere. Flowers were blooming and you could even watch as the leaves unfolded on the trees. It was hard to sit in school when the warm breezes blew in through the open windows and robins were singing just outside on a tree.

While sitting at her desk and gazing out the window, Brigitta thought of a poem and wrote:

> *Easter, Easter's here again*
> *and will bring us cheer again.*
> *Robin fellow sings so bright*
> *melts the snow that is so white.*
> *Many years of Easters*
> *but the best one's on its way.*
> *here's a wish for a Happy Easter*
> *and a very happy day!*

Well, she thought, I just wrote my first poem, even though Easter was long past.

May was dance recital month and everyone had been practicing long hours for their big performance. They wanted to be perfect in whatever they were doing.

The seamstress came in and measured them for costumes. During some of the fittings the organdy material felt scratchy, but the different colors of organdy were beautiful and Brigitta could hardly wait until the costumes were done. They all tried to be patient as they stood quietly for their measurements.

The ballet class had a special group dance to perform besides individual ones. There were acrobatic dances and tap dancing, as well. There were solo dances and group dances. There was also a big finale number when they would all be out on the stage together. Last year for the finale, due to the War, they marched on stage waving the United States flag.

Brigitta loved every minute of the excitement. The recital was to be held in the downtown Lyric Theatre on the other end of town from their dance studio, chosen because it had nice-sized dressing rooms and a stage big enough for all their performances.

Rehearsals were held. The photographer came. Brigitta's father complained of all the money spent for this recital, but he gave her mother the money anyway. Brigitta wiped her black patent leather tap shoes with a soft cloth until they shone.

Her mother painted her acrobatic slippers with gold shiny paint. That made them stiff and uncomfortable, and yet they looked very pretty and Brigette liked the way they smelled and sparkled.

In the dressing room everyone lined up for special makeup. Some students forgot the steps they had practiced or, on recital day, forgot some of their costumes; and some students got sick from stage fright and refused to go on stage. Then when the Big Day arrived, the lights came on and it was time to perform! For one night they were famous actors and actresses. It was worth all the hard work and practice that they had done throughout the year. When the audience clapped, they knew they had done a good job. For today, thought Brigitta, I got to be a famous ballet dancer!

The next day, Brigitta's mother served her favorite meal; potato pancakes. Now everyone could enjoy the summer. All too soon fall would come again, along with another season of expectations and dancing school.

Potato Pancakes

3 large peeled and shredded potatoes
2 beaten eggs
2 Tablespoons flour
dash of salt
2 Tablespoons oil

Mix the above ingredients in a bowl. Heat a griddle with oil.

Carefully pour the potato mixture one pancake at a time, being watchful that the griddle is not too hot. When the pancakes are lightly browned, serve with sugar and/or applesauce.

The end

Printed in the United States
By Bookmasters